I0820317

Combat Sports

BOXING

GAIL TERP

Bolt is published by Black Rabbit Books
P.O. Box 227, Mankato, Minnesota, 56002.
www.blackrabbitbooks.com

Rhea Magaro, designer;
Alissa Thielges, editor

Library of Congress Cataloging-in-Publication Data
Names: Terp, Gail, 1951- author.
Title: Boxing / by Gail Terp.
Description: Mankato, MN: Black Rabbit Books, [2025] | Series: Combat sports | Includes bibliographical references and index. | Audience: Ages 8–12 | Audience: Grades 4–6 | Summary: "Get ready to punch and jab with power in this hi-lo nonfiction chapter book about boxing. Reluctant readers learn about the skills and training needed to compete on both an amateur and pro level and will be inspired by champions of this combat sport"—Provided by publisher.
Identifiers: LCCN 2024011814 (print) | LCCN 2024011815 (ebook) | ISBN 9781644666821 (library binding) | ISBN 9781644667002 (ebook)
Subjects: LCSH: Boxing—Juvenile literature.
Classification: LCC GV1136 .T37 2025 (print) | LCC GV1136 (ebook) | DDC 796.83—dc23/eng/20240321
LC record available at https://lccn.loc.gov/2024011814
LC ebook record available at https://lccn.loc.gov/2024011815

Printed in the United States of America

Image Credits

Alamy Stock Photo/John Barry, 4, Taka Wu, 24, Owen Humphreys, 28 (t), Liam McBurney, 28 (b), Cal Sport Media, 29 (t), Sipa USA, 29 (b); Dreamstime/Galkin57, 24; Getty Images/Cris Esqueda/Golden Boy, 6, Elsa/Golden Boy, 9, SolStock, 16-17, Richard Pelham, 18-19, James Chance, 26; Shutterstock/Mike Orlov, cover, FOTOKITA, 1, Jomyoothphoto, 3, Master1305, 11 (t), Jacob Lund, 11 (b), 13 (m), Microgen, 12, Dario Lo Presti, 13 (t), Geobor, 13 (b), monticello, 14 (t), Happy Author, 14 (b), Andrii Zhmendak, 15 (t), Olga Popova, 15 (m), Moti Meiri, 15 (b), wavebreakmedia, 20, Sanit Fuangnakhon, 21, PeopleImages.com - Yuri A, 22-23, irin-k, 25, Tatiana Popova, 31, Wayhome Studio, 32

Contents

CHAPTER 1

The

The bell dings for **round** one. Both boxers jump up. Jab-jab-jab! The first boxer punches his **opponent's** face three times. His opponent lands a hard uppercut on his chin. The boxer falls but quickly hops up. Many times, the two fighters trade punches. Ding! End of the round.

AMERICAN EXPRESS
gopuff
Duelbits
PRIME
DAZN
BOXING
PPV
adidas

RIVAL
KING

The Win

Round two. Punch after punch, the boxers go at it. Both are getting tired.

Round three. The first boxer lands a few quick jabs. Then wham! He lands a hard one. His opponent falls to the mat. The referee counts to ten. The man stays down. It's a **knockout**!

CHAPTER 2

Getting Ready to

Boxers must be strong. And they must have **stamina**. To stay strong, they work out several days a week. Strength helps boxers hit hard. It also keeps them from getting tired quickly.

Shawn Porter is a two-time world boxing champion. He is known for his strength and fierce fighting style. He did commentary for boxing at the Tokyo Olympics in 2021.

Important Skills

Boxers practice skills over and over. Top skills include **stance**, footwork, and punching. A good stance is key for balance. Good balance means stronger punches. Good footwork is also key for balance. And fast footwork helps boxers avoid getting punched. Punching practice leads to both fast and **accurate** punches.

Boxing schools usually begin with kids around age eight.

Punches

First, boxers must learn many types of punches. Then they learn how to combine them. These combos help them land more punches.

There are four main punches. A jab and uppercut are quick snaps. The hook and cross are both power punches. A hook is delivered with a bent elbow. A cross is thrown across the body.

hook
elbow is bent

cross

cross-body punch

jab

quick, straight punch

uppercut

starts low, swings up into the chin

WHAT BOXERS NEED

GLOVES

protect hands

HAND WRAPS

worn under gloves to support fingers and wrists

HEADGEAR

protects the head

MOUTHGUARD

protects teeth and jaw

SHOES

help boxers
move better

CHAPTER 3

In the Ring

There are four basic boxing styles. Swarmers have high energy and stamina. They strike like a swarm of bees. Out-boxers move around the outside of the **ring**. They come in to hit and then move out again. Sluggers are very strong. They often win fights with a powerful blow. Boxer-punchers have a mix of the other styles. They switch styles as they need to.

BOXING STYLES

SWARMERS:
aggressive and fast

OUT-BOXERS:
quick footwork

SLUGGERS:
power punchers

BOXER-PUNCHERS:
mix of styles

Winning a Bout

The fastest way to win a **bout** is a knockout (KO). A ref can also decide if a boxer can't defend themselves. That's a technical knockout (TKO).

Many bouts are won by points. Fight judges give points for strong punches and other good moves. The winner is the one with the most points.

Boxing bouts are fought in rounds. They are two to three minutes long.

Amateur vs. Pro

There are both **amateur** and **professional** boxers. Amateurs box as a hobby or sport. They don't get paid. The pros box as a career. They get paid to box.

Men's Amateur

Women's Amateur

Men's Professional

Women's Professional

number of rounds

Ring Size

AMATEUR
16'x20' to 20'x20'

PROFESSIONAL
No set ring size

Headgear

AMATEUR	PROFESSIONAL
yes	no

NUMBER OF ROUNDS

3

4

up to 12

up to 10

1 2 3 4 5 6 7 8 9 10 11 12

By the Numbers

5,000 YEARS
how long boxing has been around

$275 million
THE MOST MONEY A BOXER HAS WON FOR ONE FIGHT

110 rounds
THE LONGEST BOXING MATCH, HELD IN 1800S

17
YEARS OLD
age of youngest boxing champion

6 to 16
OUNCES
(0.17 TO 0.45 KG)
WEIGHT OF BOXING GLOVE

adidas
MARTIN

The World Boxing Association is a professional boxing group. It holds world championship fights. Amateurs can fight in the Golden Gloves Tournament. Boxers around the United States compete.

Boxing is an event at the Olympics too. Boxers from around the world compete. Many top pro boxers start in the Olympics.

Boxer Martin Bakole once swallowed a wasp during a fight. Ouch!

Olympic Weight Classes

Boxers are matched by their weight class. Each class is labeled with its top weight. This helps make bouts fair. There is more than one weight system. The Olympic weight class system is one of them.

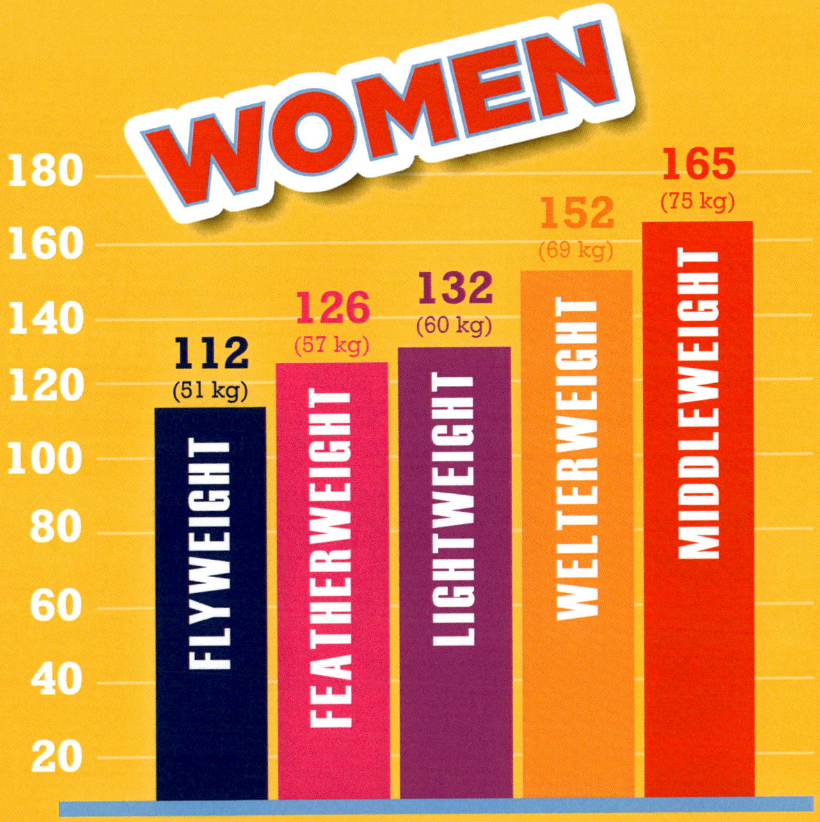

WOMEN
180
160
140
120
100
80
60
40
20
112
(51 kg)
FLYWEIGHT
126
(57 kg)
FEATHERWEIGHT
132
(60 kg)
LIGHTWEIGHT
152
(69 kg)
WELTERWEIGHT
165
(75 kg)
MIDDLEWEIGHT

MEN
210
200
180
160
140
120
100
80
60
40
20
112
(51 kg)
FLYWEIGHT
126
(57 kg)
FEATHERWEIGHT
139
(63 kg)
LIGHTWEIGHT
152
(69 kg)
WELTERWEIGHT
165
(75 kg)
MIDDLEWEIGHT
179
(81 kg)
LIGHT HEAVYWEIGHT
201
(91kg)
HEAVYWEIGHT
OVER
201
(91 kg)
SUPER HEAVYWEIGHT

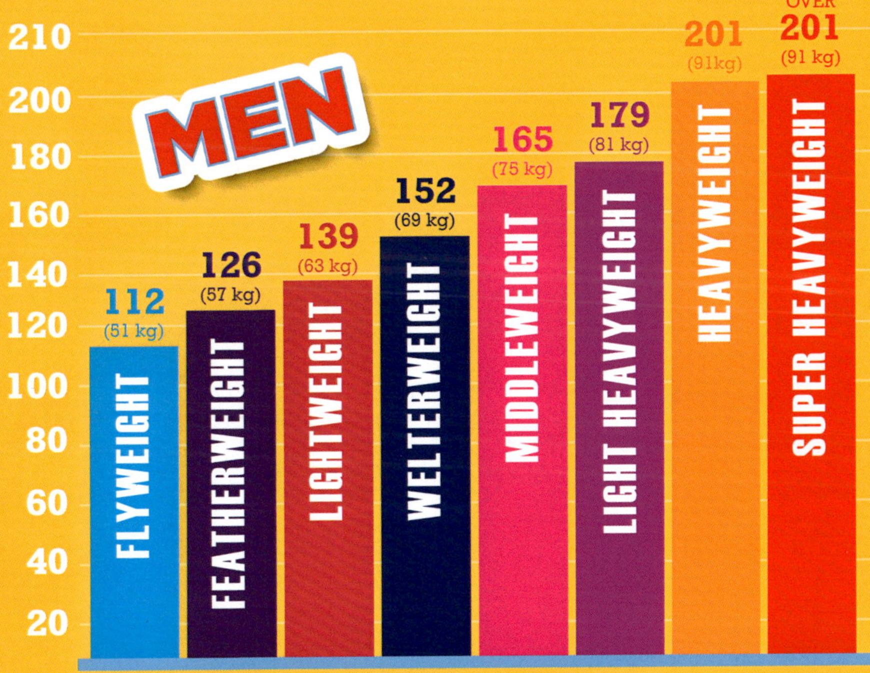

Claressa Shields

is an American pro boxer. She's won two Olympic gold medals. She's a middleweight champion.

Katie Taylor

is a lightweight champion from Ireland. She has also won Olympic gold. As a pro boxer, she fights in the United States and Europe.

American
Terence Crawford
has fought in three weight classes. He's won championships in them all.

Oleksandr Usyk
is a heavyweight from Ukraine. As a pro, he's won several world championships.

GLOSSARY

accurate (AK-yuhr-it)—free from mistakes or errors

amateur (AM-uh-chur)—not professional

bout (BOUT)—a wrestling or boxing contest

knockout (NOK-ouwt)—the end of a boxing match when one boxer has been knocked down and is unable to get up and keep boxing within a certain time

opponent (uh-POH-nunt)—a person, team, or group that is competing against another

professional (pro-FESH-uh-nuhl)—paid to compete in a sport or activity

ring (RING)—an area used for a contest or show that is usually surrounded by ropes or a fence

round (ROUND)—one of a series of similar events

stamina (STAM-uh-nuh)—the ability or strength to keep doing something for a long time

stance (STANS)—a way of standing

BOOKS

Anderson, Josh. *Muhammad Ali: Athletes Who Made a Difference.* Minneapolis: Graphic Universe, 2024.

McDougall, Chrös. *The Olympics Encyclopedia for Kids.* Minneapolis: Abdo Publishing, 2022.

Osborne, M. K. *Combat Sports.* Mankato, MN: Amicus, 2020.

WEBSITES

Boxing Facts for Kids
kids.kiddle.co/Boxing

Why Is a Boxing Ring Square?
www.wonderopolis.org/wonder/Why-Is-a-Boxing-Ring-Square

INDEX